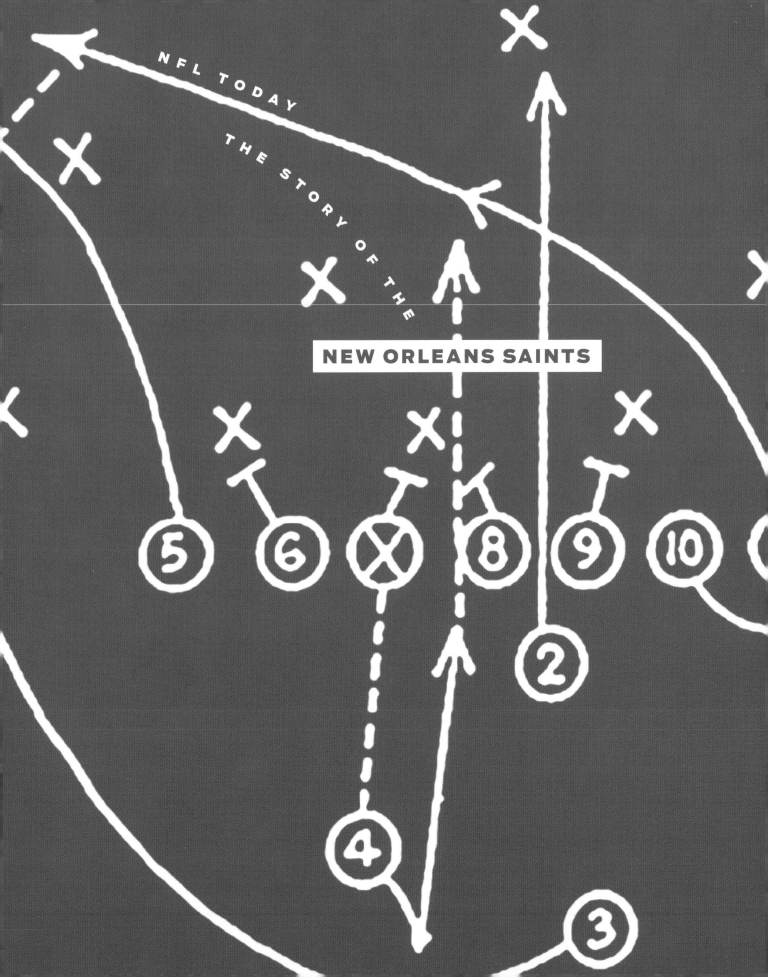

NFL TODAY

THE STORY OF THE

NEW ORLEANS SAINTS

NFL TODAY

THE STORY OF THE NEW ORLEANS SAINTS

JIM WHITING

CREATIVE EDUCATION

PUBLISHED BY CREATIVE EDUCATION
P.O. BOX 227, MANKATO, MINNESOTA 56002
CREATIVE EDUCATION IS AN IMPRINT OF THE CREATIVE COMPANY
WWW.THECREATIVECOMPANY.US

DESIGN AND PRODUCTION BY BLUE DESIGN
ART DIRECTION BY RITA MARSHALL
PRINTED IN THE UNITED STATES OF AMERICA

PHOTOGRAPHS BY CORBIS (BETTMANN, TAMI
CHAPPELL/REUTERS), GETTY IMAGES (AL BELLO,
MONICA M. DAVEY/AFP, STEPHEN DUNN, JOHN
FITZHUGH/BILOXI SUN HERALD/MCT, JAMES FLORES/
NFL PHOTOS, SEAN GARDNER, GEORGE GOJKOVICH,
CHRIS GRAYTHEN, OTTO GREULE JR., JIM GUND,
ANDY HAYT, WESLEY HITT, HARRY HOW/ALLSPORT,
JED JACOBSOHN, NICK LAHAM, STREETER LECKA,
NEIL LEIFER/SPORTS ILLUSTRATED, ED MAHAN/NFL
PHOTOS, RONALD MARTINEZ, AL MESSERSCHMIDT,
PETER READ MILLER/SPORTS ILLUSTRATED, DONALD
MIRALLE, NFL PHOTOS, MIKE POWELL, MANNY RUBIO/
NFL PHOTOS, JAMIE SQUIRE/ALLSPORT, MARIO TAMA,
TYRONE TURNER/NATIONAL GEOGRAPHIC)

LIBRARY OF CONGRESS CATALOGING-IN-PUBLICATION DATA
WHITING, JIM.
THE STORY OF THE NEW ORLEANS SAINTS / BY JIM WHITING.
P. CM. — (NFL TODAY)
INCLUDES INDEX.
SUMMARY: THE HISTORY OF THE NATIONAL FOOTBALL LEAGUE'S
NEW ORLEANS SAINTS, SURVEYING THE FRANCHISE'S BIGGEST
STARS AND MOST MEMORABLE MOMENTS FROM ITS INAUGURAL
SEASON IN 1967 TO TODAY.
ISBN 978-1-60818-311-1
1. NEW ORLEANS SAINTS (FOOTBALL TEAM)—HISTORY—JUVENILE
LITERATURE. I. TITLE.

GV956.N366W45 2013
796.332'640976335—DC23   2012031650

FIRST EDITION
9 8 7 6 5 4 3 2 1

COVER AND PAGE 2: TIGHT END JIMMY GRAHAM
PAGES 4–5: RUNNING BACK REGGIE BUSH
PAGE 6: CORNERBACK JABARI GREER

TABLE OF CONTENTS

SIDELINE STORIES

MEET THE SAINTS

THE FRENCH QUARTER IS A POPULAR TOURIST ATTRACTION IN NEW ORLEANS

Big Easy Beginnings

Sometimes numbers are deceiving. Take New Orleans, Louisiana, for example. In 1840, it was the third-largest city in the United States. By 2010, it had fallen to 52nd. Yet these figures don't do justice to the city's reputation or to its importance in American history. Settled by French fur traders in 1718, New Orleans passed into Spanish hands before becoming part of the fledgling U.S. with the Louisiana Purchase in 1803. Its key location where the Mississippi River empties into the Gulf of Mexico resulted in a savory stew of cultural influences that included African American, Creole, Cajun, Latin American, and many others.

New Orleans, nicknamed "The Big Easy," is the birthplace of jazz music and the site of the annual, world-famous Mardi Gras festival. Hundreds of thousands of tourists throng its streets every year, enjoying world-famous food and architecture in its historic neighborhoods. As award-winning television journalist Charles Kuralt once said, "New Orleans is the unique American place." Its vibrant reputation was one reason the

BILLY KILMER WAS THE NEW ORLEANS SAINTS' FIRST STARTING QUARTERBACK

Archie Manning

QUARTERBACK / SAINTS SEASONS: 1971–82 / HEIGHT: 6-FOOT-3 / WEIGHT: 212 POUNDS

The New Orleans Saints selected Archie Manning with the second pick of the 1971 NFL Draft. Manning had been a sensational quarterback at the University of Mississippi, and the Saints hoped that his strong, accurate arm would lead them to the top. But although Manning's impressive 11-year career with the Saints included two trips to the Pro Bowl and Player of the Year honors in 1978, it never once included a winning season. Among Manning's statistical achievements with the Saints—such as his 21,734 passing yards and 115 touchdowns—is an even more telling number: 340 sacks. Manning played behind an offensive line that struggled to protect the quarterback, which left him flat on his back at the end of many plays. Manning played with the Houston Oilers and the Minnesota Vikings after the Saints traded him away in 1982, but he returned to New Orleans to raise his family—including sons Peyton and Eli, who both followed in their father's footsteps as star quarterbacks in the NFL—after retirement. Today, he serves as an analyst with the Saints' radio and preseason television broadcasts.

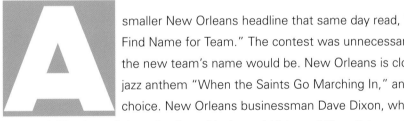

KICKER TOM DEMPSEY'S SPECIAL SHOE WAS PROVEN TO OFFER NO UNFAIR ADVANTAGE

National Football League (NFL) awarded a franchise to the city in 1966. "N.O. Goes Pro!" shouted the headline of the *New Orleans States-Item* on November 1.

A smaller New Orleans headline that same day read, "States-Item Holds Contest to Find Name for Team." The contest was unnecessary, as there was little doubt what the new team's name would be. New Orleans is closely identified with the beloved jazz anthem "When the Saints Go Marching In," and "Saints" seemed the clear-cut choice. New Orleans businessman Dave Dixon, who oversaw the team's admission into the NFL, cleared the selection with the archbishop of New Orleans. "I told him some gentlemen think somehow or another the name 'Saints' for our football team might be a little sacrilegious," Dixon said. The archbishop replied, "It's certainly not sacrilegious. Besides, I have a terrible instinct that we're going to need all the help we can get."

The team's first coach, Tom Fears, agreed with the archbishop's instinct. His ragtag roster consisted largely of aging castoffs from other teams and inexperienced rookies. At one end of the spectrum was 14-year veteran defensive end Doug Atkins, a 6-foot-8 giant. At the other end was scrappy receiver Danny Abramowicz. When receiver John Gilliam returned the opening kickoff of the Saints' first game 94 yards for a touchdown, it seemed that the team might have a chance. Despite that promising start, the

Saints lost their first seven games and finished their inaugural season 3–11.

Neither the Saints nor their fans were too disappointed. In its first few years of existence, the team cobbled together a better record than any previous NFL expansion team, and several players emerged as stars. Abramowicz was the league's top receiver in 1969, with 73 catches for 1,015 yards and 7 touchdowns. Kicker Tom Dempsey, who was born without toes on his right foot and wore a custom-made, square-toed shoe, set a team record with four field goals against the New York Giants in November 1969.

ith new coach J. D. Roberts stalking the sidelines the following year, Dempsey attempted a 63-yard field goal in the waning seconds of a game against the Detroit Lions. When his record-setting kick sailed through the uprights, and the Saints won 19–17, the players hoisted their coach in celebration. "They carried J. D. off the field like he was a hero," said Peter Finney, a longtime New Orleans newspaperman. "J. D. was on top of the world."

That was as good as it would get for the Saints under Roberts. The team lost the final six games of the 1970 season to end 2–11–1 and tallied only six more total wins in the following two seasons. Roberts was fired before the start of the 1973 season. By then, a new savior was in the Saints' sights: quarterback Archie Manning, taken with the second overall pick of the 1971 NFL Draft.

In Manning's first game, the Saints faced the Los Angeles Rams, a team they had never beaten. Manning passed for one touchdown and ran for another on the final play of the game to seal a 24–20 victory. That game set the tone for his career. During his 11 seasons in New Orleans, the quarterback would play in two Pro Bowls and set virtually every team passing record. But Manning couldn't guide the Saints to a winning record by himself.

In 1975, the Saints left behind their original home, rickety Tulane Stadium, and moved into the Louisiana Superdome, a state-of-the-art indoor facility in downtown New Orleans. Then new coach Hank Stram tried to find Manning some help. In the 1976 NFL Draft, the Saints selected fleet-footed running

Flower Power

At first glance, a flower might seem an odd symbol for a professional football team. But the fleur-de-lis, a stylized lily, is no ordinary blossom. With a history that extends back to the ancient Greeks, it became a longtime symbol of the French royal families. Famed French warrior Joan of Arc put a fleur-de-lis on her battle flags. It forms a prominent part of the logo for both the Boy Scouts of America and the Chevrolet Corvette, America's ultimate muscle car. In the aftermath of 2005's Hurricane Katrina, New Orleans residents posted crudely drawn fleur-de-lis on walls as a symbol of hope and recovery from the disaster. Virtually everyone in New Orleans recognizes the symbol and its connection to the team. Linebacker Scott Fujita said that when his two-year-old twin daughters "[saw] the fleur-de-lis around town, the first thing they [said was], 'Go, Saints!'" Team members take a fierce pride in the fleur-de-lis, which appears in six places on their uniforms. As defensive end Bobby McCray explained, "It's not like all the other logos in the NFL, like a simple animal or something like that. This is pretty distinguished."

FOR YEARS, THE SAINTS HAVE BEEN SUPPORTED BY PASSIONATE AND COLORFUL FANS

CHUCK MUNCIE (#42) RUSHED FOR NEARLY 1,200 YARDS IN 1979

backs Chuck Muncie and Tony Galbreath. Although Muncie set a club record with 811 rushing yards in 1977, the Saints remained mired at the bottom of the National Football Conference (NFC) West Division standings, with a 4–10 record in 1976 and a 3–11 mark in 1977.

Things improved in 1978. Manning threw for 3,416 yards and was honored as the NFC's Player of the Year, and the Saints enjoyed their finest season yet, posting 7 wins and 9 losses. In 1979, Muncie ran wild, becoming the first Saints player to amass more than 1,000 rushing yards in a season. That same year, speedy young receiver Wes Chandler set a club record with 1,069 receiving yards. The team finally broke even with an 8–8 record. "We're going to be there very soon," linebacker Joe Federspiel told reporters. "This town is dying for a winner, and everyone on this team is dying to be one."

Tom Benson

TEAM OWNER / SAINTS SEASONS: 1985–PRESENT

New Orleans native Tom Benson owned several successful automobile dealerships in Louisiana and Texas, which allowed him to invest in a network of local banks. But it was his multimillion-dollar investment in the Saints that made Benson famous. In 1985, as rumors circulated that out-of-state buyers might be trying to move the team, Benson bought the Saints. Benson's colorful character and love for his hometown team were soon obvious. In one game a year after buying the team, he headed down to the field to celebrate a Saints rout of the Tampa Bay Buccaneers. He congratulated players and coaches, then did a happy little dance that ended up being pictured in the newspaper. Benson did the same dance when the Saints beat the San Francisco 49ers a few weeks later, and again when they topped the Los Angeles Rams in a close 6–0 game. By then, his dance had a name: "The Benson Boogie." Fans encouraged the owner to dance, and Benson has boogied on the sidelines every time the Saints have won at home since then. "That started with a lot of enthusiasm," Benson said, "something between me and the fans."

Frustrated Fans

New Orleans Saints fans were used to losing. By the time the 1980 season started, the Saints had lost more than 125 games in 13 years. But after five consecutive losses in 1980, even stoic Saints fans were embarrassed—especially Bobby LeCompte, a local bar manager who still attended each dreadful home game. Because anyone who recognized him teased him about his loyalty to the team, he decided to hide his face at the games. He cut ear, eye, nose, and mouth holes in a paper bag, placed a Saints sticker on it, and scrawled the word "Ain'ts" across it. He and a few friends wore these bags over their heads as New Orleans lost to the Atlanta Falcons on October 19. The next week, more fans showed up wearing bags. By the time the 0–11 Saints played the Los Angeles Rams on *Monday Night Football* in November, the Superdome was full of decorated bags. Despite team attempts to ban the bags, fans continued to wear them during the dismal 1–15 season, and the idea spread to fans of other failing teams as well.

FANS EXPRESSED THEIR FRUSTRATION ABOUT NEW ORLEANS' LOSING WAYS

Ending the Ain'ts Era

The Saints' rising hopes were dashed in 1980. The club's defense collapsed completely, and the team lost its first 14 games, many by wide margins. The offense also sputtered after Muncie was traded in October. As fans and newspaper writers began calling the team the "Ain'ts," coach Dick Nolan was fired—the sixth coach to be dismissed in the Saints' 13-year history. The team filed its worst record yet: 1–15.

The 1981 season started with a new leader, former Houston Oilers coach O. A. "Bum" Phillips, and sensational new running back George Rogers, the 1980 Heisman Trophy winner as college football's top player. In his rookie year, Rogers led the league in rushing with a jaw-dropping 1,674 yards and was an easy choice as NFL Rookie of the Year.

Phillips was rewarded with a promotion to general manager in 1982, but to the dismay of the

DEFENSIVE LINEMAN FRANK WARREN PLAYED 13 SEASONS FOR THE SAINTS

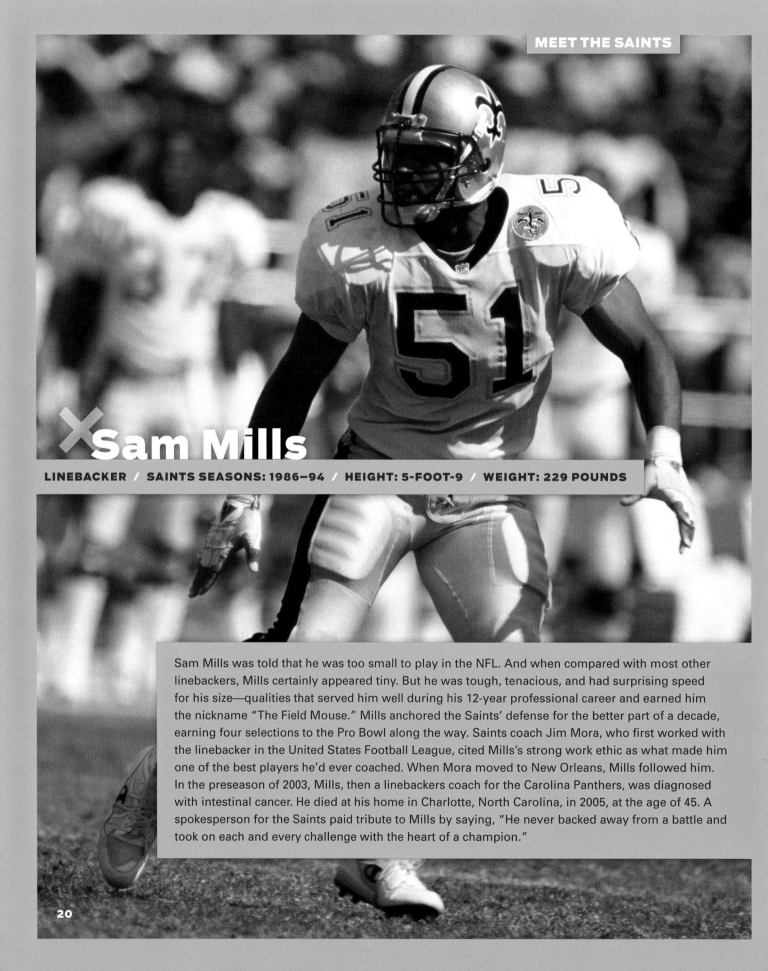

Sam Mills

LINEBACKER / SAINTS SEASONS: 1986–94 / HEIGHT: 5-FOOT-9 / WEIGHT: 229 POUNDS

Sam Mills was told that he was too small to play in the NFL. And when compared with most other linebackers, Mills certainly appeared tiny. But he was tough, tenacious, and had surprising speed for his size—qualities that served him well during his 12-year professional career and earned him the nickname "The Field Mouse." Mills anchored the Saints' defense for the better part of a decade, earning four selections to the Pro Bowl along the way. Saints coach Jim Mora, who first worked with the linebacker in the United States Football League, cited Mills's strong work ethic as what made him one of the best players he'd ever coached. When Mora moved to New Orleans, Mills followed him. In the preseason of 2003, Mills, then a linebackers coach for the Carolina Panthers, was diagnosed with intestinal cancer. He died at his home in Charlotte, North Carolina, in 2005, at the age of 45. A spokesperson for the Saints paid tribute to Mills by saying, "He never backed away from a battle and took on each and every challenge with the heart of a champion."

Saints' faithful fans, he traded Manning to the Oilers for tackle Leon Gray. Manning had grown up with the team and taken it to the cusp of competitiveness, but Phillips believed that a roster shakeup was what the team needed to leave its losing ways behind. "It broke my heart to leave the Saints," Manning said. "I don't think it had to do with Bum disliking me. I think he had a quick-fix agenda and just wanted to win right away, with his guys."

Phillips and the Saints won four games during the strike-shortened 1982 season. The next year began with Rogers breaking Chuck Muncie's single-game rushing record by racing for 206 yards in a 28–17 victory over the St. Louis Cardinals, the first of eight wins for the Saints. Unfortunately, the season ended with New Orleans just outside the playoffs, as the Los Angeles Rams kicked a game-winning field goal with six seconds left in the last game of the season. Although the Saints had yet to record a winning season, optimism was running high once again.

Defensively, New Orleans was fielding a fine team by this time. Anchored by linemen Derland Moore, Jim Wilks, Frank Warren, and Bruce Clark, the Saints led the league in pass defense in 1983 and 1984. Offensively, there were holes to fill. Management tried to plug these holes with veterans, including quarterback Ken Stabler and running back Earl Campbell. But both were in the twilight of their careers and couldn't offer the kind of offensive spark the team needed.

Coulda, Woulda, Shoulda

Jim Mora didn't walk into his postgame press conference on October 25, 1987, with a script in hand. All the New Orleans coach had was the memory of his team's bitter defeat that day, a 24–22 loss to the San Francisco 49ers that sent the Saints' record to 3–3. But that was enough to trigger one of the most motivational speeches in football history. "The Saints ain't good enough," Mora fumed. "It's that simple." He called his team "the worst franchise in the history of the National Football League" and could barely describe how upset he was. "I'm sick of coulda, woulda, shoulda, coming close, if only," he said. It wasn't just the reporters who were listening, however. His players heard every word as well—and they took it to heart. The Saints won their next nine games and ended the season with a winning record, the first time that had ever happened for New Orleans. "That's exactly what we needed," quarterback Bobby Hebert said. "The team needed a Mora personality. He gave us that speech, and we won nine straight games."

RECEIVER JOE HORN INSPIRED TEAMMATES DURING PREGAME HUDDLES

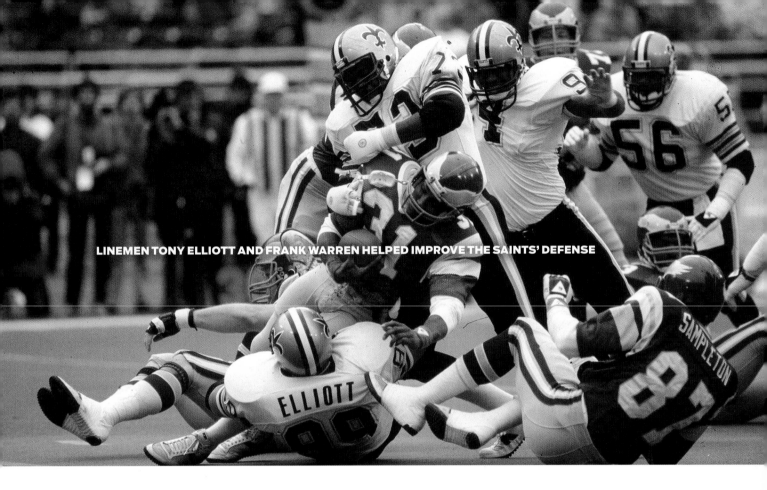

LINEMEN TONY ELLIOTT AND FRANK WARREN HELPED IMPROVE THE SAINTS' DEFENSE

The club did get a bit of a spark, though, in the form of a new owner. In May 1985, New Orleans businessman Tom Benson paid more than $70 million for the Saints. He spent even more money in overhauling the organization from top to bottom. He even tried to change the team's gold and black uniforms to blue and gold—but backed off after poll results showed that fans didn't like the idea.

However, fans did like the first head coach under Benson's watch. Jim Mora took over in 1986 and immediately started fining, benching, and cutting players until he found the right combination. Mora's sole focus was to turn the "Ain'ts" into winners. During the sweltering Louisiana summer, he put the squad to the test, running post-practice sprints until players collapsed from the heat. "I had never trained a team in that kind of heat before," he later said. "I was going to make an impression."

Mora's approach seemed to lend New Orleans a new toughness. Two decades after the Saints had begun play, all the pieces were finally falling into place. Rookie running back Rueben Mayes ran nonstop in 1986, setting team records and earning NFL Rookie of the Year honors. Kicker Morten Andersen and linebacker Rickey Jackson joined him in the Pro Bowl. But while the Saints' 7–9 record was an improvement, it wasn't quite what the team or its fans were hoping for.

The 1987 season did not start promisingly. A players' strike canceled one game and forced

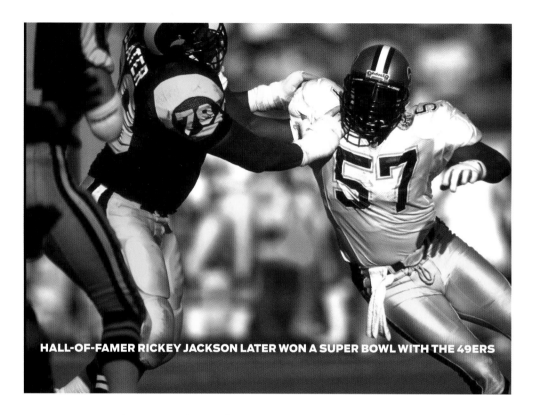

HALL-OF-FAMER RICKEY JACKSON LATER WON A SUPER BOWL WITH THE 49ERS

teams to use replacement players for three more. When the regular roster returned on October 25, the San Francisco 49ers topped the Saints in a 24–22 thriller that inspired Coach Mora's infamous "coulda, woulda, shoulda" speech about how his team just wasn't good enough to win. His emotional and heartfelt outburst triggered a response in the players. "I think that was something that shook the guys and woke everybody up," said linebacker Sam Mills. "It made the guys think, 'Hey, we've gotta get the ball rolling.'"

They did. The next Sunday, the Saints routed the Atlanta Falcons 38–0. That victory launched an unprecedented winning streak that lasted for the remaining eight games of the season. When New Orleans' bruising defense made two impressive stops of the Pittsburgh Steelers offense late in a game at the end of November to win 20–16, the Saints achieved their first-ever winning record. The next week, a victory over the Tampa Bay Buccaneers guaranteed another first: a trip to the playoffs. With an incredible 12–3 record, the Saints marched triumphantly into the postseason against the Minnesota Vikings, only to lose 44–10.

The Dome Patrol

New Orleans made the playoffs for the first time in 1987. It's probably not a coincidence that that year marked the first time that linebackers Rickey Jackson, Sam Mills, Vaughan Johnson, and Pat Swilling played together. Known as the "Dome Patrol," the foursome was later named by the NFL Network as the greatest linebacker corps in NFL history. One sign of their greatness was the fact that, after two decades without a winning season, the Saints didn't have a single losing season in the six years that the Dome Patrol remained together, and the team went to the playoffs four times. Afterward, New Orleans almost immediately reverted to its customary futility. The Dome Patrol reached its peak in 1992, when all four players were named to the Pro Bowl, the only time that has happened for four linebacker teammates in NFL history. "I think what made them so good was that they complemented each other so well," said longtime Saints blogger Andrew Juge. "Each was particularly good in one area, and it made the other guys better because as a unit they were so complete."

THE SAINTS HAVE CALLED THE LOUISIANA SUPERDOME THEIR HOME SINCE 1975

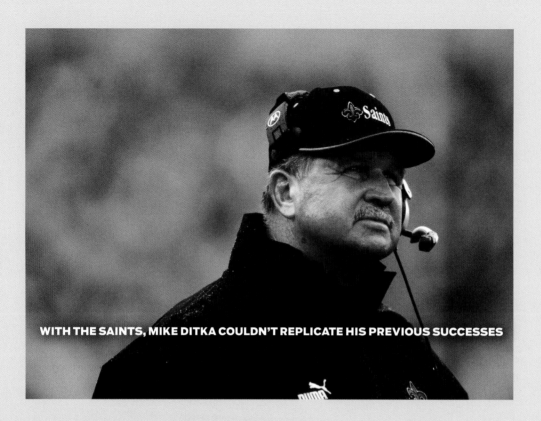

WITH THE SAINTS, MIKE DITKA COULDN'T REPLICATE HIS PREVIOUS SUCCESSES

Cajun Cannons and Iron Mikes

Despite that defeat, the sweet smell of success lingered in New Orleans. Mora was named NFL Coach of the Year, and six Saints players were voted Pro-Bowlers. The late 1980s were characterized by a defense that effectively shut down its opponents, with the help of nimble but tough linebackers such as Mills, Jackson, and Pat Swilling rushing opposing quarterbacks, tackling, and forcing fumbles. And in scrappy young quarterback Bobby "The Cajun Cannon" Hebert, the team had finally found a suitable replacement for Archie Manning. Between Hebert's strong right arm and Andersen's powerful left leg, the offense set new team scoring records.

The Saints remained near the top of the NFC standings in the seasons that followed, making the playoffs again in 1990, 1991, and 1992. At one point in 1991, New Orleans sat atop the NFC West Division with an incredible 9–1 record and a five-game lead over the 49ers. "Nine and one is beautiful," Mills remarked, "but we still have a ways to go."

LOUISIANA NATIVE BOBBY HEBERT QUARTERBACKED THE SAINTS FOR SEVEN SEASONS

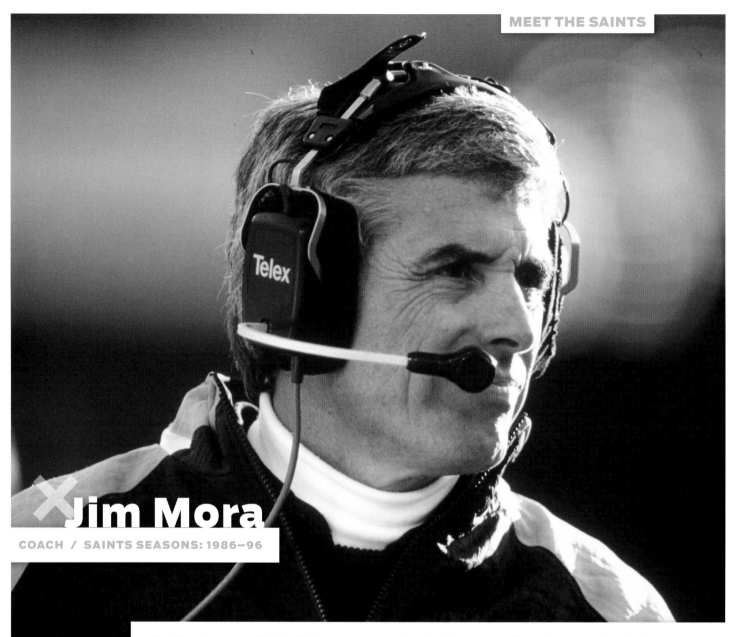

Jim Mora

COACH / SAINTS SEASONS: 1986–96

Jim Mora's career with the Saints was an emotional roller coaster. He took a team that had never recorded a winning season and led it to a 12–3 record in his second season at the helm. The Saints finished at .500 or better seven times under Mora and made it to the playoffs four times. But Mora, who was honored as the NFL Coach of the Year in 1987, often let his temper get the best of him. His emotional postgame press conferences were often laced with profanity, including the memorable "coulda, woulda, shoulda" speech that preceded the Saints' nine-game winning streak in 1987. He's also remembered for launching into a tirade after the Saints were beaten by the Carolina Panthers midway through the 1996 season—and for abruptly resigning shortly thereafter. From 1998 through 2001, Mora coached the Indianapolis Colts. At the time of his retirement from the NFL in 2001, he had compiled a career coaching record of 125–112. Ninety-three of those wins were with the Saints. Until Sean Payton came along, he was the only Saints coach ever with a winning record.

PAT SWILLING EARNED NFL DEFENSIVE PLAYER OF THE YEAR HONORS IN 1991

Mills's guarded optimism reflected what everyone in the New Orleans organization seemed to know: There was still a monkey on the Saints' backs. Every time they made it to the playoffs, they fell in the first round. The Chicago Bears beat them 16–6 in 1990. The Atlanta Falcons came from behind in the 1991 playoffs to win 27–20. In 1992, the Philadelphia Eagles scored 26 points in the fourth quarter to defeat the Saints 36–20.

Then, just as suddenly as the Saints had risen, they slid back down in the standings. After posting a 12–4 record in 1992, the Saints dropped to 8–8 in 1993. The next two years, they posted 7–9 records and disappeared from the playoff picture. As the face of the Saints changed—Swilling was traded for offensive tackle Willie Roaf, Hebert was replaced by veteran Jim Everett, and Andersen was released—so did the team's fortunes. The bottom fell out in 1996, when the Saints posted only two wins in the first half of the season.

That was the last straw for Coach Mora. On October 20, 1996, after his team suffered a 19–7 loss to the Carolina Panthers, the Saints' coach erupted in a postgame press conference punctuated with

profanity. "It was an awful performance by our football team," he said. "We should be totally embarrassed, totally ashamed." That night, Mora called Benson and gave his immediate resignation.

The 1997 Saints strutted into the Superdome with a bold new coach, "Iron" Mike Ditka, who had coached the 1985 Chicago Bears to victory in Super Bowl XX. His hiring boosted season-ticket sales but didn't lift the on-field fortunes of the sagging Saints. Ditka shuffled players in and out of starting roles throughout the 1997 season, but the inconsistent offense sputtered, and New Orleans posted 6–10 records in both 1997 and 1998. Ditka's headline-making solution was to trade eight draft picks to the Washington Redskins for the opportunity to select University of Texas running back Ricky Williams fifth overall in the 1999 NFL Draft.

Williams had been a

RICKY WILLIAMS HAD GREATER SUCCESS AFTER 2001 WITH THE DOLPHINS

Willie Roaf

OFFENSIVE TACKLE / SAINTS SEASONS: 1993–2001 / HEIGHT: 6-FOOT-5 / WEIGHT: 320 POUNDS

In seven of the nine seasons that Willie Roaf played for the New Orleans Saints, the hulking offensive lineman earned a place in the Pro Bowl. That kind of play is exactly what the Saints wanted when they drafted Roaf with the eighth overall pick of the 1993 NFL Draft. He had enjoyed an outstanding college football career at Louisiana Tech, developing the strength and quickness that would also define his professional career. Roaf became one of the best offensive linemen in the game and was a cornerstone of the Saints' offense. Unfortunately, in the middle of the 2001 season, Roaf demanded to be traded, citing irreconcilable differences with coach Jim Haslett as the reason. He was dealt to the Kansas City Chiefs, where he played for four more years and was voted to the Pro Bowl each time. Two years after his retirement in 2006, Roaf was inducted into the Saints Hall of Fame. "There aren't many offensive linemen that ever played this game who had the athletic talent that he had and all the other things, too," said Jim Mora, who coached him for four years.

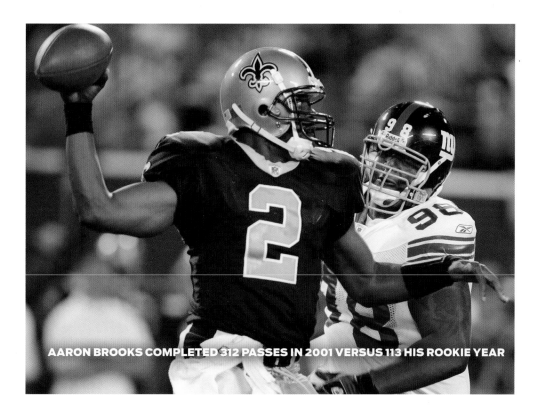

AARON BROOKS COMPLETED 312 PASSES IN 2001 VERSUS 113 HIS ROOKIE YEAR

superstar in college, rushing for 2,124 yards in his final season and winning the Heisman Trophy. Unfortunately, the halfback had too many problems—including injuries and struggles with an anxiety disorder—to single-handedly fix the Saints' offense. As the team stumbled through a 3–13 season in 1999, owner Tom Benson promised that next year would be different. "I will take whatever steps necessary to make the New Orleans Saints a winning franchise," he said.

Benson fired Ditka and hired coach Jim Haslett. Then the Saints traded for Aaron Brooks, a nimble young quarterback who had been Brett Favre's backup with the Green Bay Packers. New Orleans passers connected with speedy receiver Joe Horn a club-record 94 times in 2000 as the resurgent Saints claimed first place in the NFC West and returned to the playoffs after a seven-year absence.

When the Saints met the defending Super Bowl champion St. Louis Rams in the playoffs, Brooks threw four touchdown passes, including three to reliable receiver Willie Jackson. Special teams player Brian Milne sealed the Saints' first-ever playoff victory by pouncing on a fumbled punt with less than two minutes remaining. Even though the Saints lost to the Vikings a week later, New Orleans had finally tasted victory in the postseason, and the team was hungry for more.

The Saints missed the playoffs the following season, though, finishing 7–9. The team then gave up on Williams, trading him to Miami. The Saints struggled again in 2002, even with brawny running back Deuce McAllister racking up more than 100 rushing yards in 8 different games. Despite some terrific performances by Brooks, McAllister, and kicker John Carney, the Saints remained out of playoff contention in 2003 and 2004 as well.

JOE HORN EARNED FOUR TRIPS TO THE PRO BOWL AS A MEMBER OF THE SAINTS

DEUCE McALLISTER WAS NEW ORLEANS' ALL-TIME LEADING RUSHER AS OF 2013

One Jazzy Championship

In 2005, football became an afterthought for most of Louisiana. On August 29, Hurricane Katrina devastated New Orleans and much of the Gulf Coast region. The Superdome became an emergency shelter for thousands of residents whose homes were either underwater or destroyed. The displaced Saints shuttled between Tiger Stadium at Louisiana State University and the Alamodome in San Antonio, Texas, for home games and managed only three wins.

A bright spot in the Saints' string of bad luck was the securing of the second overall pick in the 2006 NFL Draft, with which the team selected swift running back Reggie Bush. Bush was in the backfield when the Saints returned to the Superdome for a *Monday Night Football* game on September 25, 2006. Sparked by the energetic response of fans in their recovering home city and the arm of new quarterback Drew Brees—a free-agent pickup—the Saints won that night in Sean Payton's home debut

IN 2006, DREW BREES PASSED FOR A THEN CAREER-HIGH 4,418 YARDS

Season in a Suitcase

After Hurricane Katrina ravaged New Orleans and left the Superdome in disarray, the Saints had to play their 2005 home games elsewhere. The team set up temporary headquarters in San Antonio, Texas, nearly 600 miles west of New Orleans, and made arrangements to play home games there and at Louisiana State University's Tiger Stadium in Baton Rouge. The arrangements unraveled a little in the second game, when the NFL forced the Saints to be the "home" team against the New York Giants—on the Giants' home field. Despite the obstacles, New Orleans won two of its first four games. Then the Saints' leading rusher, Deuce McAllister, suffered a season-ending knee injury, and the unsettled schedule began to wear on players. As offensive tackle Jon Stinchcomb noted, "At first we were in the Alamodome, then the waterworks building, then you're doing rehab in the press box of a high school baseball field. That's tough while you're still trying to win ballgames." Defensive end Will Smith added, "Every week we were traveling, everything was changing every week, and we never really got set in a routine." The Saints won just 1 of their final 12 games to finish a dismal 3–13.

HURRICANE KATRINA FORCED THE SAINTS OUT OF THE SUPERDOME FOR A YEAR

as head coach. New Orleans went on to finish 10–6 and won the new NFC South Division. After winning a playoff game against the Philadelphia Eagles, the Saints fell in the NFC Championship Game to the Chicago Bears.

New Orleans remained a contender in 2007 and 2008 but could not reach the postseason again. Still, the Saints were exciting to watch. Linebacker Scott Fujita led the defense, while Coach Payton directed a high-powered passing offense starring Brees, Bush, and such up-and-comers as receivers Marques Colston and Lance Moore.

Everything came together in 2009. The team started the season an incredible 13–0 before losing the final three games while resting some starters. The Saints rebounded in the postseason

BEEFY DEFENSIVE TACKLE HOLLIS THOMAS FILLED GAPS IN THE TRENCHES

The Bounty Scandal

From 2009 through 2011, the Saints' defensive coordinator, Gregg Williams, administered a system of secret—and very unsaintly—bounties. Under this system, New Orleans coaches and players contributed money to a pool. Then, Saints defensive players who deliberately injured high-profile players on opposing teams would receive cash rewards that ranged from $1,000 to $10,000 or even more. Eventually word leaked out, and the league investigated. In 2012, after considering the evidence, NFL commissioner Roger Goodell hit New Orleans with harsh penalties. For allowing the bounty system to exist, Saints coach Sean Payton was suspended for a year without pay. Williams—who by then was with the St. Louis Rams—was suspended indefinitely. The team was also fined $500,000 and lost several high draft choices. Four Saints players—most notably linebacker Jonathan Vilma—were suspended for parts of the 2012 season, but their suspensions were later overturned. "I am profoundly troubled by the fact that players—including leaders among the defensive players—embraced this program so enthusiastically and participated with what appears to have been a deliberate lack of concern for the well-being of their fellow players," Goodell said.

SAINTS DEFENDERS INCURRED MANY ROUGHING-THE-PASSER PENALTY FLAGS

MARQUES COLSTON CAUGHT SEVEN PASSES IN SUPER BOWL XLIV

TRACY PORTER'S PERFORMANCE HELPED CLINCH THE SAINTS' TITLE

to thrash Arizona 45–14, then knocked off Minnesota 31–28 in overtime in the NFC title game to advance to the Super Bowl for the first time in team history. With the devastation of Katrina still fresh in the minds of many people throughout the country, the Saints were the sentimental favorites in Super Bowl XLIV against the Indianapolis Colts. "Look around the stadium," said Fujita. "It was like 6- or 7-to-1 [Saints fans]. The black and gold just poured into Miami. The whole world was behind us."

Down 10–0 in the first quarter, the Saints scored two field goals to trail 10–6 at halftime. After recovering an onside kick to start the second half, New Orleans took a 13–10 lead. A Brees touchdown pass and two-point conversion gave New Orleans a 24–17 advantage with less than six minutes remaining in the fourth quarter. Then, with the Colts threatening to score, Saints cornerback Tracy Porter intercepted a pass and romped 74 yards to cement a 31–17 Saints win. "We just believed in ourselves, and we knew that we had an entire city and maybe an entire country behind us," said Brees, who was named Super Bowl Most Valuable Player (MVP). "What can I say? I tried to imagine what this moment would be like for a long time, and it's better than expected."

New Orleans returned to the playoffs the following year as a Wild Card team with an 11–5 record. But the Seattle Seahawks—a team that had earned ridicule for winning the NFC West with a mere 7–9 record—rode the momentum of a raucous home crowd to knock off the defending champions 41–36.

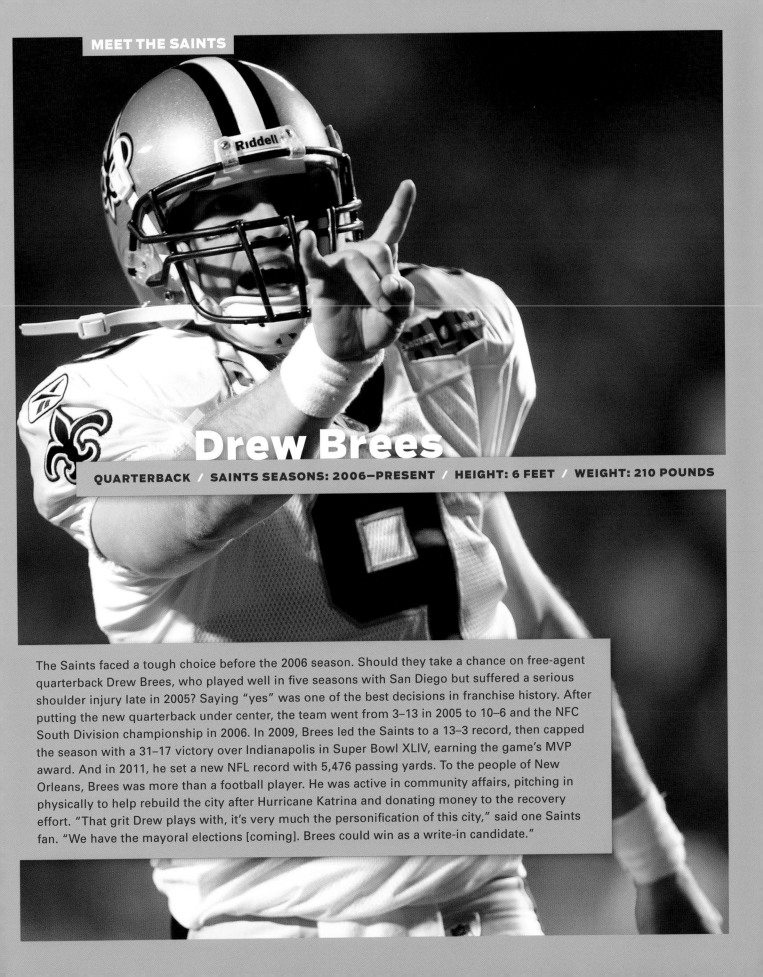

Drew Brees

QUARTERBACK / SAINTS SEASONS: 2006–PRESENT / HEIGHT: 6 FEET / WEIGHT: 210 POUNDS

The Saints faced a tough choice before the 2006 season. Should they take a chance on free-agent quarterback Drew Brees, who played well in five seasons with San Diego but suffered a serious shoulder injury late in 2005? Saying "yes" was one of the best decisions in franchise history. After putting the new quarterback under center, the team went from 3–13 in 2005 to 10–6 and the NFC South Division championship in 2006. In 2009, Brees led the Saints to a 13–3 record, then capped the season with a 31–17 victory over Indianapolis in Super Bowl XLIV, earning the game's MVP award. And in 2011, he set a new NFL record with 5,476 passing yards. To the people of New Orleans, Brees was more than a football player. He was active in community affairs, pitching in physically to help rebuild the city after Hurricane Katrina and donating money to the recovery effort. "That grit Drew plays with, it's very much the personification of this city," said one Saints fan. "We have the mayoral elections [coming]. Brees could win as a write-in candidate."

RUNNING BACK DARREN SPROLES HAD A CAREER YEAR FOR ALL-PURPOSE YARDS IN 2011

PRO FOOTBALL WAS IN HEISMAN TROPHY WINNER MARK INGRAM'S FAMILY

Despite flashes of brilliance, Bush had never quite lived up to the lofty expectations the Saints had for him, so they selected powerful University of Alabama running back Mark Ingram with their top pick in the 2011 NFL Draft. "He's physical," said Coach Payton. "He's got great balance." With Ingram added to the mix, the 2011 Saints won their last eight games of the year to again capture the NFC South. But after topping the Detroit Lions 45–28 to open the playoffs, New Orleans fell to San Francisco 36–32 in a thrilling game that saw four lead changes in the final four minutes.

New Orleans hoped to become the first team to play in a Super Bowl on their home turf as the 2012 season opened. However, such hopes were jeopardized by the scandal known as "Bountygate," which left the team without head coach Sean Payton for the entire season and without his replacement, Joe Vitt, for the first six games. Though the Saints managed to claw back into playoff contention by early November with a 5–5 mark, their subsequent three-game losing streak (which resulted in their first losing season since 2007) ended any realistic Super Bowl chances. Statistically, Brees had one of his best years, throwing for 5,177 yards and 46 touchdowns. "To have gone through what we went through this year and just to hang tough … it would have been very easy at times to fracture and not have the togetherness that we had," Brees reflected. "Sean's going to come in chomping at the bit and we're going to have to be ready to roll."

In the last half decade, the once-woebegone "Ain'ts" have transformed themselves into one of the NFL's elite franchises. As today's Saints do gridiron battle in The Big Easy, visiting teams find nothing easy about earning a victory in New Orleans. And when the Saints do capture their second Super Bowl championship, historic old New Orleans will echo with music and celebration once again.

INDEX